MY *SECRET* LIFE

a friendship with God

Margaret Hebblethwaite

Illustrated by Peter Kavanagh

MOREHOUSE PUBLISHING
Harrisburg, PA   Wilton, CT

I have a secret life, a life just to myself.
I hide away sometimes, all by myself, and no one
knows what I am doing.

No one, that is, except for a
very special person.
He is a secret person, but not
a pretend person.

He is real, but you
cannot see him.

He is God.

I have secrets with God.
I talk to him. I tell him things that I do not tell anyone else.

I like having secrets with God.

When God and I want to have secrets together,
we like it best when no one else is around.

We like it best when we can just be quiet together,
and not have anyone else burst in.

In the summer I go and hide
in the garden. In my garden there is
a big bush with lots of leaves.
Sometimes it has big, yellow flowers
as well, and...

...they smell lovely.

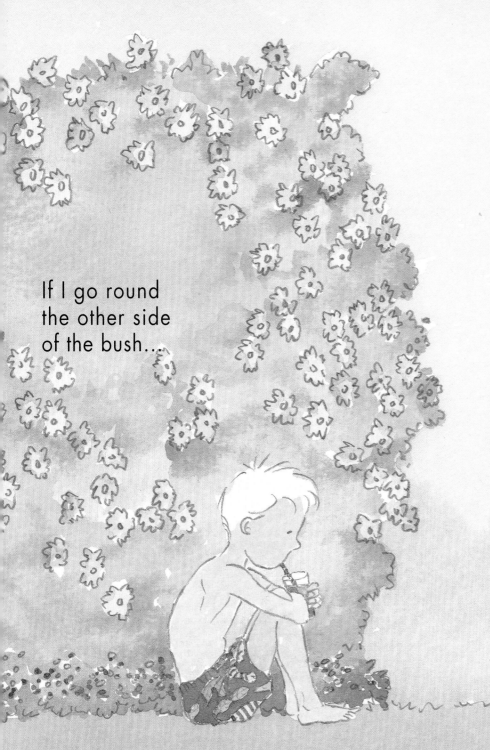

If I go round
the other side
of the bush...

...no one can see me.

My mother can look out of the
kitchen window and not
even know if I am in the
garden or not.

So I like going behind my
bush and sitting on the
grass there.

I can talk to God there, and
know that no one else is
watching me.

When it is cold or rainy I can't go behind my bush, but there are other places to go.

We have a little room at the top of our house called the attic, with lots of boxes and old things in it, like my father's crash helmet that he doesn't use because he doesn't have a motor bike any more, and the dress my mother wore when she got married.

8

Sometimes I go up there
when I want to be
alone with God.

There are lots of memories up there.
Most of them are not my
memories, because I am too
young to have such old
memories, but they are
God's memories, and I like
to be where God has memories.

When my mother doesn't let me go to the attic because she says
I will get dirty, then I have other places for my secret life.

Sometimes I hide round the back of the sofa in the living room.

It is cosy there, on the blue carpet underneath the window, with the light falling into my secret place, and the high wall of the sofa back making a little house for me.

I think God likes it there too, because it is light and comfortable, but it is not quite as secret as the other places if I want to have a long talk to God.

Another place where I go to
be alone with God
is in my bedroom.

God always stays with
me when I am asleep
so he is used to
being there.

He likes my bedroom
because it really is
my place.

If I prop up my bedding over the end of the bed
I can make a tent, and then take a book
under the tent for me and God to
look at together.

I have a book about mountains that I like to show to God,
and then we pretend we are in a tent up a very
high mountain-side on an exciting expedition.

Outside is a raging snowstorm,
but inside the tent I am
safe and warm
with God.

Sometimes when I haven't even gone into a secret place I still have my private talks with God.

Sometimes I have them when we are out in the car or when the grown-ups are talking at mealtimes, and no one even knows I am having my secret life with God.

I just talk to God silently, without opening my mouth.

I talk to him in my head, with my thoughts,
and God understands everything I am saying.

God always understands everything I want to
tell him, and he knows everything I have done,
but he doesn't ever tell my secrets.

What sort of secrets do I tell God?

Well, I tell him all kinds of things.

Sometimes I am sad
because my mother has
shouted at me,
and my father has said
he is busy,
and my sister has said she
doesn't want to play with me.

So then I tell God I am sad.

Or sometimes I do not even tell him — he just knows anyway.

After I have been sad with God for a while I feel better, because he understands why I am sad even when I cannot explain it very well.

That is one kind of secret we have together.

I also tell God my secret wishes.

You know that when you pull a wish-bone and you get the bigger bit you can have a wish?

Sometimes it comes true, and sometimes it doesn't.

18

But did you know that with God you can have wishes all the time,
not just when you win at pulling the wish-bone?

And did you know that a wish you ask God for is much more
likely to come true than a wish with a wish-bone?

You didn't?

What a lot you have been missing!

19

Sometimes God
makes me wait for a
while before he gives me
what I ask for. But there
are lots of things that he has
given me.

I asked for a bike for my birthday
and I got that. And I asked for a ride
in my uncle's new red sports car and
I got that. And I asked for my teacher to give
me a 'very good' in my workbook and I got that.

There are one or two more things I have
asked for that I haven't got yet,
but you never know,
they might come tomorrow.

But God likes it best if the things
you ask for are not all for yourself.
So I asked for my father's bad back to
get better, and it did, after a while.

And I try to remember to ask things
for people I don't know, too.

Once I heard of some children whose
parents died in a car crash,
so I asked God to help them.

I bet he did.

Another thing God likes is when
you say thank you.

So that is another of my
secrets with God.

I say thank you
for all my
best things.

I thank him for my mother and my father and my sister and my
friends. I thank him for my house and my garden and my bike.
Sometimes when I have got something I want, I forget
that I had asked God for it.
So I do not always remember to say thank you, but I
try to remember.

If I have forgotten for quite a while
I say 'sorry' and 'thank you'
together.

Thank you for the thing I asked
for, and sorry I haven't
said 'thank you' before.

I also say sorry if I know I
have done something wrong,
like when I have told a lie.
But I know God understands
why I have told the lie, so
that makes me feel better
about saying sorry.

Another thing I talk to God about is what I want to do when I grow up.

When I become a grown-up I would like to be an Olympic athlete and win all the races. I haven't told my mother and father about that, or my friends at school, because they might say I was silly.

But I talk to God about it, because he never thinks I am silly.

I think God thinks it is
a great idea.

But he thinks lots of other
things are great ideas too,
things I have never thought of.

I think if God wants me to
be an Olympic athlete
then he will help me
become one.

And maybe he does want it
— who can say?

Anyway, whether I become an Olympic athlete or not,
I don't want to have a boring life like a lot of grown-ups.

I don't want to waste masses of time sitting around
talking and pretending to be
important and never having
any fun.

And I don't want to be as mean
as a lot of grown-ups, always
complaining how poor they
are and never giving any money
to people who are a lot poorer
than them.

So I tell God about how
I don't want to grow
up like that, and
I think he agrees.

27

I also talk to God about how I would like to be when I am just a bit older.

At my school there is a boy called Ben, who is in the next class from me.

Whatever he is doing always seems to be fun, and everyone likes to play his games.

He doesn't just play with people in his own class, but he has friends all over the school. And when he has snacks he always shares them.

He doesn't even seem to mind sharing, he seems to like it.

I am rather different from Ben.

I get bad moods sometimes,
and I get impatient when
smaller children are in
the way, and I don't
really enjoy sharing.

So I ask God to make me
more like Ben.

Maybe not all at once,
and not completely like him of course,
because I like being me.

And that brings me to the really best bit about my secrets with God.

God likes me being me, too.

He must do, because he made me, and he can do anything, so he would not have made me how I am if he did not like me that way.

He made me with blond hair and fond of racing because that is the way he likes me, and he knows best.

In fact God does not just like me, he really loves me.

He loves me more than anyone else does, even more than my mother and father do.

He loves me even when I am quarrelling with everyone else, and nothing is going right for me.

And he wants to see me happy and having a good time.

So the really, really best bit of my secret life with God is knowing just that —
—that he really loves me, and wants me to have my secret life with him.

So often all we do, God and I, is do nothing together.

If you are with someone as fantastic as that, you don't need to say anything very much.
You just enjoy being together, as friends.

And God is my best friend of all.